Combat Sports

BY M. K. OSBORNE

WITHDRAWN

AMICUS | AMICUS INK

Amicus High Interest is published by Amicus and Amicus Ink
P.O. Box 1329, Mankato, MN 56002
www.amicuspublishing.us

Library of Congress Cataloging-in-Publication Data
Names: Osborne, M. K., author.
Title: Combat sports / by M.K. Osborne.
Description: Mankato, Minnesota : Amicus, [2020] | Series:
  Summer Olympic sports | Includes bibliographical references
  and index. | Audience: K to grade 3.
Identifiers: LCCN 2019001947 (print) | LCCN 2019003011
  (ebook) | ISBN 9781681518626 (pdf) | ISBN
  9781681518220 (library binding) | ISBN
  9781681525501 (pbk.)
Subjects: LCSH: Hand-to-hand fighting–Juvenile literature. |
  Martial arts–Juvenile literature.
Classification: LCC GV1111 (ebook) | LCC GV1111 .O73
  2020 (print) | DDC 796.8–dc23
LC record available at https://lccn.loc.gov/2019001947

Editor: Wendy Dieker
Designer: Aubrey Harper
Photo Researcher: Shane Freed

Photo Credits: Kyodo/AP/KYDPL Kyodo cover; Hahn Lionel/
AP 4; Kyodo/Newscom 7; Paul Sancya/AP 8-9; Markus
Schreiber/AP 11; Wang Haofei/Newscom 12; Frank Franklin
II/AP 15; Felipe Trueba/Newscom 16; Fotoarena/Alamy
19; Jae C. Hong/AP 20; Actionplus/Alamy 22-23; Fabrizo
Bensch/Newscom 24; Dominic Ebenbichler/Newscom 27;
Mutsu Kawamori/Newscom 28

Printed in the United States of America

HC 10 9 8 7 6 5 4 3 2 1
PB 10 9 8 7 6 5 4 3 2 1

Table of Contents

Pads and uniforms make today's combat events look different than they did in ancient times.

Q When were the first Olympics held?

Ancient Events

The Olympic Games are some of the oldest sporting events in the world. The very first Olympics were in ancient Greece. The games featured wrestling, boxing, and an early form of **martial arts**. Those combat sports made their way to the modern Summer Games. Fans can't wait to see who will win the gold medal in these events.

 The very first Olympic Games were held in 776 B.C. The games we know today started in 1896.

Wrestling

Two wrestlers step onto the mat. They circle each other. One wrestler strikes! She takes down the other woman. She holds the woman's shoulders to the mat. It's a **pin**! This is wrestling. The rules of wrestling have changed a little since ancient times, but the basics are the same. Wrestlers use strength and power to win the match.

Helen Louise Maroulis of the U.S. takes down Saori Yoshida of Japan in a wrestling match.

A big wrestler could easily win against a smaller one. To keep matches fair, wrestlers are grouped by weight. They only take on those of the same size.

Athletes wrestle for two periods. Each period is three minutes long. The match ends if a wrestler pins his or her opponent.

Athletes from France (blue) and Cuba (red) wrestle for a bronze medal in 2012.

The Olympics features two kinds of wrestling. Men compete in Greco-Roman style. It is much like the ancient sport. Wrestlers can use only their arms and upper bodies for **holds**.

Both men and women compete in freestyle wrestling. Wrestlers can use their arms or legs to make a hold.

 Which country has the most wrestling medals?

Freestyle wrestlers try to gain control with both arms and legs.

 The Soviet Union does. It is no longer a country. Yet it still holds the record with 132 medals! The United States is second with 128.

Olympic boxers always wear
red or blue uniforms.

Boxing

Ding! The bell rings. Round one begins. Olympic boxing has always been a hit. Both men and women face off in the ring. Just like in wrestling, weight classes keep fights even. A heavy fighter won't step in the ring with a smaller person. Men battle it out in eight different weight classes. Women have five. The top two boxers in each class fight for the gold medal.

Boxers go toe-to-toe in three rounds. Rounds are three minutes long. Boxers score points by landing punches. Big punches get higher scores. Matches don't always go to the end of the round. They sometimes end with a **knockout**. That's when a boxer gets punched hard and falls to the mat. If the **ref** counts to ten, the match is over.

Boxers from China (red) and the Netherlands (blue) fight to earn a spot in the next match.

Tae kwon do means "the way of the fist and foot." The feet are what score big points.

Martial Arts

The Ancient Greeks loved watching early martial arts. Fighters combined wrestling and boxing. Today's Olympic Games features fighting sports from around the world.

Tae kwon do comes from South Korea. Men and women thrill fans with their fights. They have hard punches and big kicks.

Tae kwon do starts with a bow. But then the fight starts. Kicks get the most points in these matches. Each kick has a point value. Straight kicks to the body are worth 2 points. A straight kick to the head is worth 3 points. Spinning kicks are worth 4 points to the body and 5 points to the head.

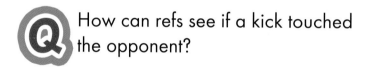 How can refs see if a kick touched the opponent?

Judges and refs carefully watch tae kwon do matches to give scores.

 They get help from sensors on the trunk pads. These sensors help count kicks and punches electronically.

Gold medalist Kayla Harrison of the U.S. (top) pulls out of a judo hold in 2016.

 Why don't judo fighters wear pads?

On another mat, a different kind of fight is happening. This is a judo match. These fighters have no pads. One athlete grabs the other. They **grapple**. They throw each other around. Fighters don't score points by punching or kicking. Instead, they use holds and throws.

 Judo is a Japanese martial art called "the gentle way." Fighters do not use weapons or strikes, so they don't need padding.

A judo match lasts five minutes. The fighters try to score an **ippon**. This is a throw that lands an opponent on his or her back. The fighter who made the throw wins the match automatically. A fighter can also win by getting a submission. This is when the opponent gives up because they are in a painful hold.

A throw that lands a fighter on his back always ends the match.

Fencers have turned sword
fighting into a precision sport.

Fencing

The first sword fight probably happened right after the first two swords were invented. Today, sword fighting is an Olympic event called fencing. The swords are light and thin. The fencers are quick. They lunge to attack. They block attacks with a flick of the wrist.

Fencing looks dangerous. But pads and helmets protect the fencers. A fencer earns a point for touching the other fighter.

The Olympics features three types of fencing. Each is named for the kind of sword used. Fans see foil, épée, and saber fights. In all three events, the fencer with the most points wins.

 Why do fencing masks light up?

Electronic fencing gear protects the fighters and helps judges score matches.

Fencing masks and vests have sensors. When the sword touches them, the mask lights up.

Fighters compete in a world karate championship to prepare for the Olympics.

Bring on the Olympics!

Combat sports are exciting to watch. New for the 2020 Olympics, fans will get to watch karate. Karate is an old Japanese martial art. It's fitting to be featured in Tokyo, Japan.

Sit back and enjoy! Cheer on your favorite athletes as they fight for a gold medal!

Glossary

grapple To grab an opponent and try to make a hold or pin while avoiding getting held or pinned.

hold In wrestling and judo, a way of stopping an opponent from moving and attacking.

ippon In judo, a move to throw an opponent to the mat; an ippon ends the match.

knockout In boxing, a punch that knocks an opponent unconscious; a knockout ends the match.

martial art A kind of fighting that originated as a form of self-defense.

pin In wrestling, to force an opponent's back flat against the mat.

ref Short for referee; the person who judges a match and makes sure the rules are followed.

Read More

Faust, Daniel. *Ibtihaj Muhammad: Muslim American Champion Fencer and Olympian.* New York: PowerKids Press, 2018.

Herman, Gail. *What Are the Summer Olympics?* New York: Penguin Random House, 2016.

Nussbaum, Ben. *Showdown: Olympics.* Huntington Beach, Calif.: Teacher Created Materials, 2019.

Websites

BBC Bitesize | How did the Olympic Games begin?
www.bbc.com/bitesize/articles/z36j7ty

Official Site of the Olympic Movement
www.olympic.org

Index

About the Author

M. K. Osborne is a children's writer and editor who gets excited about the Olympics, both the Summer and Winter Games, every two years. Osborne pores over stats and figures and medal counts to bring the best stories about the Olympics to young readers.